PRESENTATION SKILLS

THE ULTIMATE GUIDE
TO DELIVERING THE PERFECT PRESENTATION

PATRICK EBBS

ISBN: 978-1-910662-16-8

First published in 2015

TABLE OF CONTENTS

COMMUNICATION

USEFUL TOOLS AND RESOURCES

Chapter 1
INTRODUCTION

Why Go Through The Pain
Of Becoming A Great Presenter?

INTRODUCTION

25 years ago, I gave my first formal presentation and it was a disaster! I left, saying to myself "never again". I then decided to go on a journey culminating with this book. Since that day, I have undertaken extensive research into what makes a great presenter, observed numerous speakers and learned what to do and what not to do. For the past 20 years, I have been a member of Toastmasters International, a world leader in communication and leadership development. I founded ChangEnable, a consultancy that, among other services, provides presentation skills training. I have devised many training programmes and delivered them throughout the United Kingdom and Europe. I mentor and coach many clients. I am also involved in training the next generation of speakers, fifteen thousand 15-17 year olds, through the Speakers Trust's Challenge Programme.

This book encapsulates the essential elements you need to be a great presenter. It includes the most beneficial modules from the feedback on the workshops I run. It is aimed at both the novice speaker, to equip them with all the necessary tools as well as the more experienced speaker to ensure that they are presenting to the best of their ability. The novice should read the book from start to finish, whereas the more experienced speaker may decide to jump to a chapter that interests them.

This book will equip you with the essentials for success enabling you to prepare, structure and deliver effective presentations that you and your audience will enjoy.

It is divided into the following key sections:

Structure:

Having a proper structure lays the foundations for a successful presentation. It helps the presenter organise the talk so it flows smoothly and provides the audience with a route map allowing them to easily understand and get the message. Outlined in detail are the key ingredients of how to effectively structure a presentation.

Delivery:

This section outlines how to become verbal, vocal and visual. It shows how to use your voice with vocal variety so you sound interesting and engaging, helping you to deliver a lively performance. We look at body language and how gestures, movements and mannerisms can enhance, or diminish our message. Using pauses in presentations can be powerful, yet we tend to fill our pauses with filler words, the most common being Um and Ah. We will look at methods to eliminate these fillers. The last chapter in this section outlines strategies to overcome the fear of presenting in public so you appear confident and in control.

Techniques:

The Rule of Three is a tried and tested technique used by most experienced speakers as it helps to make their message memorable. Examples are provided to highlight how extensively and successfully the Rule of Three has been used. Humour is another great weapon in your speaking armoury, so I have included some ways of making your audience laugh.

Developing Your Skills:

This covers the dreaded (and most challenging) type of public speaking - impromptu speaking, known as speaking off the cuff. Using impromptu speaking to become more effective in meetings is also included.

Communication:

This section includes listening skills, a key skill for everyone - not just presenters. We then look at how to handle question and answer sessions to ensure they enhance rather than derail your presentation.

Useful Tools and Resources:

How to evaluate presentations and give feedback to other speakers is included – something which benefits both giver and receiver. A Preparation/Evaluation checklist is included to ensure all the key points are covered, in order for you to deliver a great presentation or an evaluation.

Many people fear public speaking. They would choose to do almost anything else rather than stand up to address a crowd. These are normal, intelligent, happy and well-balanced people. They appear confident and 'normal' yet, when asked to stand up and speak in public, they are struck with fear. They fear being judged by others, they fear an audience gazing at them, they fear they will make mistakes, forget their words or feel embarrassed. Panic can set in. So, many people try their best to avoid the whole thing. So if you have a fear of public speaking, you are certainly not alone! It is important to say up front, that all audiences want their presenter to succeed and will be willing them on to deliver a great presentation. Audiences attend in the hope that they will be informed, inspired, persuaded or entertained - not to sit through a poor presentation.

So why should we become effective presenters? Why should we face the fear of presenting – what's in it for us? Firstly, being a good presenter brings numerous benefits which are outlined in the next paragraph. Secondly, the good news is that we can all learn, develop and improve our presentation skills, vitally important in today's world. It does however take some effort. Firstly, practice, whether you are a novice or a professional. It is often said that 'Practice makes Perfect' or 'Practice makes Permanent'. You need to practice in order to become a confident and compelling speaker, but practice using effective techniques such as, good structure and body language. My mantra is Preparation, Preparation, Preparation and you will come across it more than once throughout this book – you have been warned!

So what are the benefits of becoming a good presenter? The value of developing your presentation skills, far outweighs the initial effort you will need to make. Even if you do not need to give regular presentations, once you learn the skills, you should seek opportunities to use them and refine them. Possessing effective presentation skills can help to advance your career and enhance your reputation.

Some of the benefits of becoming a good presenter include:

- Great leaders are usually great communicators – you become more credible, persuasive and inspirational. Think of leaders you admire and consider their communication skills
- Win more sales pitches and new business – you communicate more clearly and know how to effectively structure your message
- Your reputation is enhanced as you get noticed – sadly there are many poor presenters but when you present well, this helps you get noticed, and promoted
- Become good at it – you will be called upon to do more presentations and colleagues and friends will seek your input
- Become a better listener – as you develop your presentation skills you become a better listener
- Become a better negotiator – better able to convey your ideas, proposals and arguments
- Perform better at meetings – you know when to speak, what to say and how to say it
- Improved performance at interviews – better able to sell yourself and advance your career
- Become more confident and have greater self-belief
- Add a useful life skill to your skill set

It is well worth the pain but are you up for the challenge?

Good presentation skills are vital for many roles in today's business world. They are also important beyond the business world. For example, you may be asked to talk at a family celebration, make a best man or father of the bride speech at a wedding or give a eulogy for a loved one. Furthermore, you may have to inspire a group of colleagues or a hobby you have where effective interaction is required.

Be warned! Not all occasions when you are invited to speak in public will be planned in advance. You may be called upon to give an impromptu talk where there is no time to prepare but this book will equip you with the tools to do this effectively.

In summary, being an effective presenter can enhance your reputation, boost your self-confidence, and open up numerous opportunities.

Finally, I wish to sincerely thank all those who have contributed to this book, some knowingly and others unknowingly. This is through the feedback on content and delivery I have had after my own presentations, the hints and tips shared, the exchange of ideas from participants on my training workshops, as well as exchanges with those I mentor. I have also learned a great deal from observing others – what to do and what not to do.

May your journey begin!

Chapter 2

HOW TO GET AN OBE

The Route To A Successful Presentation

STRUCTURE

STRUCTURE: HOW TO GET AN OBE

Introduction

This is not about the Queen's Birthday Honours list; in this instance it covers the **O**pening, **B**ody and **E**nding of a speech. It's all about structure! By ensuring you have an Opening, a Body, and an Ending, you will lay the foundations for a successful presentation.

Before you begin, ask yourself *"what is the purpose of making this presentation"*? You should know exactly what you want to say and the order in which you want to say it. This will ensure it is well structured and will enable your audience to get your message. Before you start to draft your speech, you should be able to write down your purpose in less than ten words. If you are unable to, then reflect and reconsider your speech purpose. If you are not crystal clear, how will your audience get your message?

It is also important to decide what to include and what to leave out. Your content should be determined by two factors:

i) Timing

Prepare your presentation for the time you have been allotted and do not go over time. Remember to include time for questions and answers if you plan to have them. Audiences and event organisers do not mind if you finish a little earlier than planned but are not very forgiving if you go over time.

ii) Information

You may have lots and lots of information to share on your subject hence the reason you were perhaps asked to present on it. However, the amount of information audiences can digest is limited so do not overload them as they may switch off and remember very little. You are presenting to deliver your message, not to demonstrate how much you know about the subject.

Key to a successful structure is Preparation, Preparation, Preparation!

The Opening is to hook the attention of your audience. We will look at what creates a good opening and outline some opening techniques.

The Body should maintain the level of interest achieved in your Opening. Again we will look at some techniques that enable a logical sequence to be followed.

KEY TIP

When preparing for your presentation, always ask yourself the question *"What is the purpose of my presentation?"* The aim is to always ensure the audience 'get your message'.

For the Ending, think of your first sentence then your last and bring them as close together as possible. This is one method used but we will consider some other techniques to ensure you finish your presentation on a high.

An easy tried and tested method is to think about the news programmes where the newsreader tells you what he is going to tell you (Opening), he tells you (Body) and then he tells you what he just told you (Ending).

Opening

An effective opening catches your audience's attention and generates interest in your subject. Make the audience curious about your very first words, you need to grab their immediate attention. Pause before you speak, make eye contact, look confident, smile so as to engage and connect with your audience.

A successful opening should have:

Audience Attention

As you begin speaking your audience may be thinking about the awful journey they had on the way to the event, the important meeting after your presentation, or they may be chatting with their colleagues. Their attention needs to be refocused on you. A good beginning draws their attention to you and to your presentation.

Establish Rapport

Your audience will be more receptive to you and your message if you appear friendly, engaged and interested in them and show passion for your subject. Smiling, displaying enthusiasm and making eye contact are effective ways to establish rapport with your audience. When it is a familiar audience you can use names.

Introduce the Topic

The beginning of your presentation should indicate what you will be talking about and why your audience should be interested in it. What is the purpose of your presentation and what is in it for them? Most members of any audience usually ask themselves *"What's in it for me"*? So when listeners understand the topic and how they will benefit from listening to your presentation, they will immediately tune in.

Less than 5%-10% of Speech

An opening should take less than 5% to 10% of your presentation. The majority of the time should be devoted to the body.

Opening Techniques

Importance of the Topic

Tell your listeners why the subject is important to them. For example, in a speech about the dangers of too much sun, you could begin by saying *"a golden tan may be glamorous, but overexposure to the sun can age your skin prematurely and can cause skin cancer. Thus, it's important to protect yourself from the harmful rays of the sun"*.

Make a Startling Statement

Alarm your audience with an intriguing statement that will compel them to listen further. The more dramatic or even provocative it is, the more you will grab their attention. For example *"Experts warn that the number of fatalities due to obesity may soon, for the first time, exceed those caused by smoking"*.

Imagine

Inviting your audience to imagine gets them immediately hooked and involved. Each audience member is free to paint their own vivid pictures in their mind; you give them an open invitation. Your invitation to imagine must be related to your presentation purpose and help your audience get the message.

Arouse Suspense or Curiosity

Compare these two openings:

i) *"Good evening, I'm Patrick Ebbs and my aim is to give some clues on what foods to avoid so you can have less disease and less stress".*

ii) *"Would you like to add ten quality years to your life? Then think before choosing fatty foods. I'm Patrick Ebbs and you will leave today with ten easy proven steps to add those ten years to your life".*

Tell a Story or Anecdote

Telling a dramatic, emotional or humorous story or anecdote arouses interest and commands audience attention. Be sure to keep the story relevant to the main point of the presentation. Personalise it whenever possible as audiences love to hear personal stories. For example, instead of beginning *"Two men were driving in the country"*, say *"My wife and I were driving in the country"*.

Keep your story relatively short so as to get to the point, otherwise your audience will become disengaged.

If you use a humourous anecdote ensure it is appropriate for the point you wish to make and that it is not offensive.

Ask a Rhetorical Question

Opening with a question immediately moves your audience from being passive to being engaged. You can ask one question or a series of questions that relate to your presentation subject. This technique gets your audience engaged and thinking about the purpose of your talk; they will think about an answer and thus your subject. For example, in a speech about first aid, you could begin by asking: *"Do you know what to do if your child starts to choke"*?

Begin with a Quotation

Using a quotation is an easy and effective way to attract immediate attention. For example, if you were giving a motivational speech, you could start with the following quotation:

> *"Our greatest weakness lies in giving up. The most certain way to succeed is always to try just one more time".*

Thomas A Edison

Used properly, a quotation can add authority to your presentation, amuse your audience or dramatise the point you are making. Learn the quotation off by heart so you do not have to read it. Ensure that your quotation is credible, relevant to your presentation and appropriate for your audience.

It is important to pause after using any of the above opening techniques. This will help your listeners consider what you might be about to share with them.

KEY TIP

Begin your presentation with confidence, authority and control – not with excuses.

Examples of What Not to Say

Your opening needs to create interest, you need to hook your audience so do not use your opening to repeat the title of your presentation.

Do not start your presentation with an apology. Begin confidently and assertively.

Do not explain why you think you were asked to present. Have self-belief and demonstrate it.

Here are three examples of poor openings I often hear speakers use:

"I'm nervous so please bear with me"

The audience then observe your nervousness. They may feel some sympathy but they ignore your message.

"I'm sorry but I did not have time to prepare for this presentation"

The presenter is basically saying that they do not care about their audience.

"I'm delighted to be here today"

And? What is your message? This is what the audience start to ask themselves so you immediately lose them.

Examples of What to Say

Here are three examples of good openings used by top speakers:

"Imagine your business in ten years' time"

Invites the audience to create a mental image and gets them immediately involved.

"Have you ever experienced.....?"

"If I were to ask you....."

Notice that the poor examples all begin with 'I' (the presenter) and the good examples all contain 'you' (the audience). Using 'you' is an effective technique to help make your presentation about your audience.

KEY TIP

Your presentation should be more focused on 'you' and not 'I'. It's all about your audience!

The Body

The body should follow a logical sequence with frequent signposting, leading the audience through your presentation.

You have to work to keep the audience engaged. Here are some techniques to add interest to the body:

- **Questions:** throughout the body of your presentation you can involve your audience by asking for a response. An alternative is to ask a rhetorical question for a change of emphasis. For example, *"do you believe it was right to agree to sell the business"*? Or the rhetorical question, where the presenter poses a question and then answers it himself: *"You may be wondering why we have decided to sell the business................ The reasons are..............."* The rhetorical question avoids getting bogged down in discussion and losing focus.

- **Examples:** are an excellent way of keeping attention and interest and are particularly useful to illustrate a point. When used, the example should be a typical and not an exceptional one – your audience must easily 'get it'.

- **Statistics:** are a simple yet powerful way to arouse curiosity. If used, be sure that they are meaningful and relate to your presentation purpose. Do not confuse your audience; statistics are most effectively presented by using visual aids or a handout.

Transitions

Smooth transitions between each of your presentation sections will help make your talk flow in a logical sequence. They will enable the audience to stay alert and understand what is coming next. Transitions take you from your opening into the body of your presentation and provide a smooth passage between your main points. Here are some examples:

Bridge Words

The simplest transitions are bridge words – words that alert your audience that you are changing direction or moving onto a new thought. Various types of transitions can be used, examples include:

- Between similar points: Similarly, Likewise;

- Between contrasting points: However, On the other hand;

- To show the cause/effect relationship: Therefore, Consequently;

- To expand on an idea: In addition, Furthermore;
- To support an example: For example, To demonstrate this;
- To move from the Body of your presentation to your Ending: To summarise, In conclusion.

Question

A question can serve as a good transition. The question can be broad or quite specific.

Point by Point Transition

For example, *“there are three important reasons the new product will sell in Europe*" and then listing them is a quick way to shift from generalities into specifics.

Pausing

Pausing is a non-verbal transition that helps your audience move with you.

Handing over to another presenter

For example in a team presentation, *“To provide you with a demonstration of this, I will now hand over to …..”*

The Ending

> *“A speech is like a love affair – any fool can start one but to end one takes considerable skill”*
>
> Lord Mansfield

With your ending you should aim to:

Achieve a Sense of Closure

A presentation without a proper conclusion is like a joke without a punch line. Your audience ask themselves *"Is that it?"* Your audience will expect closure.

Summarise Your Key Points

An effective conclusion summarises the key points outlined in your presentation. Repetition reinforces your message.

Make an Impact

A good ending makes a lasting impression on your audience. People remember the last thing they hear. End on a high!

Takes Less Than 5% to 10% of the Entire Presentation

A brief ending reinforces your message and makes it easier for your audience to remember it.

Closing Techniques

Most of the techniques outlined for the opening can also be used for your ending. Here are a number of methods you can use to close your presentation:

Tell a Story or Anecdote

A powerful story or anecdote can make a memorable close. We covered this point in the opening techniques.

Use a Quotation

Used properly, a quotation can add authority to your closing. Use a quotation to encapsulate your message.

Call for Action

If the aim of your presentation is to persuade your audience to take some kind of action, your closing comments should be clear and specific. Your audience should be in no doubt what you are asking of them. What specific action do you want your audience to take? It should be based on the arguments you have outlined in your presentation.

KEY TIP

Structure your presentation so that the:

Opening is 5-10%

Body is 80%

Ending is 5-10%

Ask a Rhetorical Question

We have covered this in the Opening techniques. For example *"You may ask, can we afford to do this? I ask can we afford not to?"*

Refer to the Beginning of your Presentation

Link your closing words to the beginning of your presentation. This is the tried and tested method of 'tell them what you are going to tell them; tell them, then tell them what you have just told them' (like the news programmes).

In summary, good presentations require strong, logical structures so consider using the above points when preparing your next presentation.

Chapter 3

VOCAL VARIETY

Transforming An Ordinary Presentation Into An Exceptional One

DELIVERY

VOCAL VARIETY

Introduction

Effective use of vocal variety can transform an ordinary presentation into an exceptional one. Every word you use in a presentation is important, so choose them carefully to make the greatest impact. It is, of course, not only what you say but how you say it. Your tone of voice is an important part of your equipment which can bring vocal variety to add emphasis and bring life to your presentation.

How do you want to make your listeners feel? Excited, inspired, informed, persuaded, entertained or, sleepy and bored? Boring people are usually boring because of their voice and how they speak. When we encounter boring people we usually tune out. If you speak on a monotone your listeners will switch off.

People often use the excuse that they were born with their voice; it is part of who they are. This is understandable, but many of these same people were born with other features but they manage to change them! A dynamic speaking voice is an asset and in business it is crucial!

Characteristics of Vocal Variety:

The characteristics of vocal variety can be summarised with the 7 'P's:

Number 1: Pitch

Vary the pitch of your voice or, conversely, avoid the monotony of the same pitch. Imagine that you are telling a story to a child. They will not continue to listen if you talk in a monotonous tone. Seek to entertain by use of voice, and body language. Make people enjoy listening to your voice by adding variety.

The way you say something can affect the meaning. Use a lower pitch when making an important point. When you raise the pitch, it conveys energy and excitement. Raising the pitch of your voice at the end of a sentence turns a statement into a question. If you listen to the announcer reading out the classified football results on a Saturday afternoon you will notice that they change their pitch to indicate the score.

Number 2: Pace

Vary the pace of your speech. Speed up to show enthusiasm and excitement. Slow down when you want to emphasise important points. A constantly slow pace will make the audience 'switch off'. If you speak too fast, your audience is unlikely to understand you, will become frustrated and again they will "switch off." You do not wish to be accused of 'sameness' where you speak at the same pace. Use variety, change the pace and add pauses. Try listening to the commentator of a sporting event such as a football match. You do not have to understand the words they are saying to know when something exciting is happening.

Number 3: Pause

Pause after important points. The audience will listen more intently and have time to reflect on what you have just said. Furthermore, the use of pauses allows your audience to stay with you; if they are unable to keep up with you, they will simply switch off. Use pauses instead of 'um' and 'ah'. Use pauses after you have made a point or are about to change topics. Use a pause if you have just shared a story, told a joke, or even forgotten what you were going to say next! The use of pauses is also very useful for creating dramatic effect. Silence conveys confidence, control and authority. Silence is power!

Number 4: Projection

Each member of your audience should be able to hear you without any difficulty, no matter what size of venue you are in. Engage your listeners, not by being loud, but by using more breath and greater intensity. Speaking too loudly is just as bad as speaking too softly. A low but audible voice can be as effective for emphasis as speaking in a loud voice, depending on the point you are making. Emphasising a few words adds interest and emphasis to your whole presentation. Talk to them, not at them.

Number 5: Passion

Be sure to be passionate about your subject. If you do not show any passion, why should your audience?

KEY TIP

Your speech content may be impressive, it is just what your audience wants - but unless you vary the tone of your voice you will not engage them.

Number 6: Posture

Good posture helps you have an effective speaking voice. For example, if you slouch or stand with your shoulders slumped; it will reduce the power of your voice. Stand with your feet shoulder width apart and shoulders back. Good posture not only helps you breathe better but you will also look more confident.

Number 7: Practice

Practice and preparation are the best ways to improve and get comfortable using vocal variety – Preparation, Preparation, Preparation! Before you present, try and warm up your voice; you would not rush straight into physical exercise without first warming up. Saying tongue twisters is an effective voice warm up exercise.

Tongue Twisters

Good articulation helps you to speak more distinctly, so in order to improve your articulation practice by repeating tongue twisters. See some tongue twisters on the next page to get you started.

TONGUE TWISTERS

Eddie had edited it.

His story is now history.

Give papa a cup of proper coffee in a copper coffee cup.

Which witch wished which wicked wish?

Which wristwatches are Swiss wristwatches?

Rhys watched Ross switch his Irish wristwatch for a Swiss wristwatch.

A pleasant place to place a plaice is a place where a plaice is pleased to be placed.

If Pickford's packers packed a packet of crisps would the packet of crisps that Pickford's packers packed survive for two and a half years?

She is a thistle sifter, and she has a sieve of sifted thistles and a sieve of unsifted thistles, because she is a thistle sifter.

If you're keen on stunning kites and cunning stunts, buy a cunning stunning stunt kite.

One-one was a race horse. Two-two was one too. One-one won one race. Two-two won one too.

Patrick produced the perfect product for people to practice to perfect their professional presentation prowess.

Can you can a can as a canner can can a can?

I wish to wish the wish you wish to wish, but if you wish the wish the witch wishes, I won't wish the wish you wish to wish.

The Duke paid the money due to the Jew before the dew was off the grass on Tuesday, and the Jew having duly acknowledged it said adieu to the Duke for ever.

As I was in Arkansas I saw a saw that could out saw any saw I ever saw saw. If you happen to be in Arkansas and see a saw that can out saw the saw I saw saw I'd like to see the saw you saw saw.

If one doctor doctors another doctor, does the doctor who doctors the doctor doctor the doctor the way the doctor he is doctoring doctors? Or does he doctor the doctor the way the doctor who doctors doctors?

I take it you already know of tough and bough and cough and dough
Others may stumble, but not you on hiccough, thorough, slough and through
Well done and now you wish perhaps to learn of less familiar traps.
Beware of heard, a dreadful word that looks like beard and sounds like bird
And dead: it's said like bed not bead, for goodness sake don't call it deed.
Watch out for meat and great and threat, they rhyme with suite and straight and debt.
A moth is not a moth in mother, nor both in bother, broth in brother.
And here is not a match for there, nor dear and fear for bear and pear.
And then there's dose and rose and lose, just look them up and goose and choose.
And cork and work and card and ward, font and front and word and sword.
And do and go then thwart and cart, come, come I've hardly made a start
A dreadful language? Why man alive! I'd mastered it when I was five!
And yet to write it the more I try I'll not learn how 'til the day I die.

Chapter 4

BODY LANGUAGE

It's Not What You Say,
It's The Way That You Say It

DELIVERY

BODY LANGUAGE

Introduction

Body language is a key element in communication. Our physical appearance, posture, eye contact, facial expressions, movement and gestures, all influence audience perception – whether we like it or not.

Body language, sometimes referred to as non-verbal communication, can be defined as those gestures, movements and mannerisms we use to communicate with each other. The way we talk, walk, sit and stand is telling.

It's Not What You Say....

Take a look at the two paragraphs below:

Paragraph 1: You are busy in the kitchen cooking the supper. Suddenly, your partner says, *"Do you love me?"* You continue preparing the food, you do not look over at your partner and you eventually mutter the words, *"Of course, I love you."*

Paragraph 2: You are busy in the kitchen cooking the supper. Suddenly, your partner says, *"Do you love me?"* You stop preparing the food and put the utensils down. You walk across the kitchen and sit down beside your partner, take them by the hand, look them in the eyes and say, *"Of course, I love you."*

Notice that the same words are used above, but which do you think conveys the more powerful message?

It's not what you say, it's the way that you say it!

Body language plays a key role in helping us get our message across. The importance of body language is partly why peace talks are conducted face to face, so that people can fully understand each other. In public speaking it is how you interact with your audience. Body language conveys moods and emotions, and can emphasise what you say. It can however, also contradict what you say. Like it or not, your audience will interpret and react to the nonverbal signals you give during your presentation.

When we are unsure about what the person is saying, we pay more attention to the 'non-verbals'. Your body language and voice can reinforce, or equally, destroy your message. The impact on your audience comes mainly from your tone of voice (vocal variety) and your body language.

Text messages can be confusing, because they rely only on the words, with no body language or voice to communicate the message.

It is very difficult to deliver a convincing presentation by just relying on your script, PowerPoint, flipcharts or props. So your challenge is to become visually interesting. You, the presenter are the most important visual aid. Gestures, movement and facial expression play a key role in helping your audience understand and get your message. You are the one visual element of your presentation which remains on view throughout your entire presentation. Your visual and auditory signals show your audience more clearly how you feel about your subject than your words.

Speaking is like song and dance; your words and movement should be in unison. Gestures, along with your movements need to be smooth, deliberate and natural. Movement and gestures are performed to reinforce your message.

Apart from its importance when presenting, body language is also crucial for leadership effectiveness. For example, the way it can reinforce a leader's ability to lead, inspire, negotiate, manage change and build relationships. In business, these first impressions are crucial. As is often said, you never get a second chance to make a first impression!

Effective use of body language enables leaders to develop positive business relationships and to inspire and motivate their employees. They are able to present their ideas with greater influence and clarity.

KEY TIP

When presenting do not just rely on the Verbal, remember to also use the Vocal and Visual.

Be aware that your nonverbal signals do not always communicate what you intend. For example, you may be slouching because you are tired, but people interpret this as a lack of interest. Some people are more comfortable standing with their arms folded across their chest, but this is perceived by others as resistant and unapproachable.

Emphasise rather than Distract

Begin to use gestures to emphasise your message, but not distracting mannerisms. Try to avoid distractions in your presentation. I am sure that you have witnessed presenters with irritating or distracting mannerisms. They take your attention away from what they are saying and you focus more on their mannerisms. Do not let the messenger get in the way of the message.

Examples of distractions include:

Swaying or rocking motion

This can be from side to side or front to back and makes you appear nervous. Swaying is very distracting and can undermine even the most interesting presentation. Instead, plant yourself to the floor, especially at the start of your talk.

Moving around the floor too much

You should move for a reason, otherwise it can simply be a distraction. One reason to move is in order to create a timeline. For example, if you were describing your youth, then the present day and then the future, you would start on your right (please note this is your audience's left) then move to the centre of the stage for the present day and then to your left for the future.

Another reason to move is when you are describing an action or scenario. Your movement can be done slowly or at speed, depending on the specific action. Examples are:

- If you are repeatedly going to visit your sick relative
- If you are trying to lose weight but are continuously going to the fridge

In summary, move for a purpose. Your movement should be planned and deliberate.

Outfit not appropriate for the event

The audience will judge your appearance along with your credibility, knowledge and confidence. You can never be over dressed for the occasion so unless informed otherwise it is best to dress smartly. Dress to impress!

Staring at notes, screen, floor or ceiling

Nervous presenters tend to look everywhere except at their audience. Eye contact is an important feature in getting and retaining attention and engaging with your audience. Eye contact is also a good source of feedback for the presenter; is your audience engaged, interested or bored? Eye contact is more than just fleeting glances at members of the audience. It is spending time with each person so each person feels like you are just talking to them. Your whole audience will then feel that you have genuinely connected with them and you will come across as more interesting, engaging and personable.

Slouching

Stand tall with your shoulders back and look confident, despite perhaps being a nervous wreck on the inside. Slumping can also adversely affect your voice projection. Good posture also demonstrates authority and confidence.

Hands in Pockets

Presenting with your hands in your pockets can give the impression that you are insecure or, alternatively, that you are arrogant. You should be using your hands to enhance your message. For example, if you are trying to make an important point, you may hold a finger up, so do not have them buried away in your pockets. Another common distraction is the sight and sound of presenters jingling coins in their pockets.

Hands Free

Do not hold anything in your hand that you are not using. Some presenters hold a pen or marker in their hands as a comfort. If you need to use a marker, pick it up, use it and then put it down. Try to keep your hands free, get used to presenting without markers or pens in your hands. Make your hands enhance your message.

Another simple yet effective use of your hands is when you put your palms up or down. If you speak while holding your palms up, it can indicate uncertainty or it can indicate you are making an open statement. Use palms up when you are introducing yourself, or inviting a response from the audience. Palms down indicate authority, certainty or closed statements. Use palms down for definitive statements when you do not wish to invite any audience response.

Try this exercise of describing an event. Tell someone about an event that really interested you – initially with your hands clasped behind your back. Half way through, release your hands. Does the story improve? Do you feel more animated?

In summary, a mannerism is a gesture which has become a habit and the more the presenter does the gesture, the more meaningless it becomes and ultimately it distracts the audience from the content of the talk.

Ensure your body language is aligned to the words you are presenting, to add another layer of communication, to enhance your message. Do not allow your body language to become a barrier between you and your audience. Distracting mannerisms can become such a barrier.

Seeing is Believing

It is often said that a picture paints a thousand words, and the same can be said for gestures. We can subconsciously give out signals which reveal our true feelings, through our movements and gestures. The pictures below highlight poor body language and also demonstrate the effective use of it.

A relaxed, straight posture will convey confidence and authority to your audience. Slouching shows that you are nervous or disinterested. What messages are the above presenters conveying?

Your posture will attract or distract, shift or hold your audience's attention. Displaying authority and control instils confidence in your audience and helps to put them at ease. Make your first impression a powerful one!

The woman above with her arms folded may suggest that she is feeling vulnerable or nervous, so she protects herself by folding her arms. This position can also make someone appear defensive or unapproachable. The presenter with her open arms appears more open, inviting, engaging and interested.

Audiences expect presenters to be enthusiastic – does having your hands in your pockets demonstrate enthusiasm? Hands in pockets can also signal apathy, a lack of interest, insecurity or arrogance. The presenter on the right above, is much more open and engaging. Who would you rather listen to?

To engage and connect with your audience and make them feel comfortable simply begin with a smile. Before you say a word make eye contact and give a warm smile. Which of these two presenters look more inviting?

To be a successful presenter you must deliver your message most effectively using your words, voice AND body language.

Whether we like it or not, people judge us by:

- How we look
- What we say, and
- How we say it.

Hopefully, this chapter has highlighted how important our body language is to effectively ‘get our message across’. Your challenge is to become visually interesting.

Chapter 5

HOW TO ELIMINATE FILLER WORDS

Speak But Do Not Say Um Or Ah

DELIVERY

HOW TO ELIMINATE FILLER WORDS

Introduction

Using excessive filler words is an irritating presentation habit. These are a distraction which can make presenters appear unprepared, lacking in confidence and credibility, resulting in their audience switching off. They contribute nothing, and weaken your effectiveness as a presenter and can ultimately result in your message being lost.

The most common filler words are 'Um' and 'Ah' but other examples frequently heard are:

You know

Obviously

So

Like

It's like

Basically

Okay

Kind of

Right

Yeah

Well

Footballers when taking penalty kicks are trained not to look at the goalkeeper, but focus on where they are about to kick the ball. If they make eye contact with the goalkeeper they are more likely to miss the spot kick.

When presenting, filler words are the goalkeeper; concentrate on them and you are more likely to say them. Pauses are you focusing on where you are going to shoot; focus on them and you are more likely to get through your presentation with lots of effective pauses and thereby less filler words.

Thankfully, filler words can, and should be eliminated from your presentations. Here are some useful tips to help you to reduce or eliminate 'filler' words – so that you can speak but not say 'Um' or 'Ah'.

Be Aware of Fillers

To eliminate the filler words, you first have to be aware that you are using them. Many presenters, often do not necessarily notice that they frequently use filler words. Presenters are sometimes amazed when told the number of times they have used filler words in their presentations. It can often be a high number! So, it is important to be aware of your use of 'Um' and 'Ah', or any other filler words. Get your presentations evaluated and ask for your 'Um's and 'Ah's to be counted with the aim of reducing and then eliminating them.

Master the Pause

Most novice presenters are reluctant to use pauses. They tend to speak too fast due to nervousness. Alternatively, they believe their audience will think they have forgotten their presentation if they pause to think of what to say next. Instead of pausing, they use filler words to avoid the silence. Never be afraid of the silence; a pause is much more impressive than a filler word. Listeners know that you are thinking, trying to find the right word. Audiences respect this; it also allows the audience to digest what you have just said. The use of pauses shows self-confidence and the message is delivered more effectively. What can seem like a long pause to you as the presenter, is usually a short time to those in the audience.

KEY TIP

Never be afraid of the silence – learn to use more pauses throughout your presentation. The use of the pause is powerful.

Preparation Preparation Preparation

Key to building confidence is being prepared. If you know your subject thoroughly and have fully rehearsed your presentation, your delivery will go more smoothly. Rehearse – practice really does improve performance. The number of filler words tends to increase when the presenter is under prepared and under rehearsed. They can be a by-product of a lack of preparation or lack confidence in the delivery of the presentation. Preparation, Preparation, Preparation!

There are times when we do not get the opportunity to prepare. For example, many times at business meetings or even in conversations, unexpected questions come up that were not anticipated or prepared for in advance. This is when filler words are particularly prone to crop up.

Impromptu Speaking

Practising impromptu speaking (thinking on your feet) is a great training method for the above types of situations. You learn the skill of thinking on your feet, gathering facts in your head and expressing them coherently. Just like learning any new skill (scoring from the penalty spot), it takes practice to become adept at impromptu speaking (see sections on Impromptu Speaking).

Learn to eliminate your filler words to have greater impact in your presentations and enhance your communication skills.

Chapter 6

HANDLING THE FEAR

You Can Do It

DELIVERY

HANDLING THE FEAR

Introduction

I said right at the start of this book that most people fear speaking in public; it is how we handle and control the fear that is important. Athletes are nervous before an important event. Professional footballers are nervous before a big game. Actors experience stage fright. Professional, experienced presenters are nervous. You are not alone! They all have butterflies in the stomach; the key is to get those butterflies flying in formation. They provide the adrenaline to enhance your performance. Channel your nervous energy into your performance.

Nervousness is normal. Learn to accept some level of anxiety. Remind yourself that even the most seasoned presenters experience some nervous tension before they perform. A little nervousness can help you deliver a better performance. However, if you are too nervous, you may lose control and your anxiety may spread to your audience.

> *"There are two types of speakers: those that are nervous and those that are liars".*

Mark Twain

Here are some strategies to overcome the fear and get the butterflies flying in formation:

Audience Support

Firstly, remind yourself that your audience want you to succeed. If you do make a mistake, your audience will usually forgive you. Start off knowing that your audience are on your side. Think of presenting as talking to individuals, say your friends, all at the same time.

KEY TIP

Always bear in mind that audiences want you to succeed, they are on your side.

Preparation Preparation Preparation

If you knew that every time you presented you would give an excellent performance – would you be nervous? Preparation, Preparation, Preparation! Be fully prepared and be confident that you are fully prepared. Your nerves are usually worst at the start of presentations, so memorise your opening so you get off to a confident start. Being fully prepared, gives you confidence and helps mitigate the fear of presenting in front of an audience. The time and effort you commit to preparation will pay dividends in your confidence when you stand up to present.

Familiarisation

Reduce your anxiety by becoming familiar and comfortable with the presentation venue. Get there early and walk around the room and get comfortable on the stage. If you are using any audio or visual equipment, ensure that it works in order to avoid any technical problems when you present.

It is useful if you can get an opportunity to talk to some members of the audience before you present. This can help you relax as you can see some familiar faces in the crowd when you start to present.

Positive Affirmation

Repeat positive affirmations quietly to yourself. Examples are, *"I am a great presenter"*, and my personal favourite, *"I can and I will."* Focus on the positive stuff, not what can go wrong.

Visualisation

Before any presentation I perform, part of my preparation routine is to visualise it beforehand. I imagine myself walking confidently to the lectern, my immediate connection with the audience and delivering a great opening. As I continue, I can see that the audience is fully engaged, enthused and enjoying it. I end on a high and leave the stage to warm applause. I recall this positive image and tell myself that I have already given this performance (in my mind) so I have nothing to fear when doing it for real.

If visualisation sounds a little touchy feely for you, then replace it with mental preparation.......Preparation, Preparation, Preparation!

Breathe

Taking slow, deep breaths, breathing out fully and then in again, will help relax you. There are numerous relaxation exercises available online, so discover what works best for you. I relax my facial muscles by opening my mouth and eyes wide, and then closing them tightly. When appropriate (i.e. not in front of the audience!) I vigorously shake my hands about.

KEY TIP

Memorise your opening to get off to a confident start.

Posture

Stand tall, with your shoulders back and chest out. Smile. You may not feel confident on the inside but try and give your audience the impression that you are.

Smile

Perhaps not easy when you are nervous, but do remember to smile. Firstly, it will help relax both you and the audience. Secondly, it conveys a confident person which will help give you a greater sense of control and authority.

Grab every opportunity to present. Start off in familiar surroundings with people you are comfortable with. Then move out of your comfort zone and find more challenging engagements. Do not wait to be asked to present – volunteer. It becomes easier through preparation, practice and by doing it. The only way to do it, is to do it. So, feel the fear and do it!

Chapter 7
THE RULE OF THREE IS POWERFUL

The Most Persuasive Number
In Communications

TECHNIQUES

THE RULE OF THREE IS POWERFUL

Introduction

The Rule of Three is a technique that can be found in many of the greatest speeches. It is no coincidence that the number three is generally used in stories, fairy tales and brand marketing. Furthermore, some of the most famous historical quotes are structured in three parts. The Rule of Three is used because it flows nicely, it is easy for the listener to remember without feeling overloaded and because it feels complete.

It is an effective presentation technique and one that you should learn to incorporate into your presentations. Using the Rule of Three allows you to communicate your ideas with greater clarity, emphasise your points, and help reinforce your message (yet another example of this!). The Rule of Three says that three key messages is the optimal number for maximum audience recall.

There are numerous examples of the Rule of Three:

Brand Straplines

- Nike – Just Do It
- Heinz – Beanz Meanz Heinz
- John Lewis – Never Knowingly Undersold
- Mars – Work, rest and play
- ChangEnable – together YOU can!

Films, TV & Books

- The Good, the Bad, and the Ugly
- Ready, Steady, Cook
- Location, Location, Location

- The Three Musketeers
- The Three Little Pigs
- Goldilocks and the Three Bears

Christianity

- The Father, Son, and Holy Spirit
- Faith, Hope and Charity
- Three Wise Men with their gold, frankincense, and myrrh

Politics

- US Declaration of Independence: "Life, liberty, and the pursuit of happiness"
- French motto: Liberté, Égalité, Fraternité
- The number of tri-coloured flags

Problem Solving

When presenting on problem solving ask what is the:

- Issue?
- Resolution?
- Outcome?

Other

- The Olympic motto: Faster, Higher, Stronger
- Blood, sweat and tears
- Preparation, Preparation, Preparation!

KEY TIP

The Rule of Three is powerful. That's the truth, the whole truth, and nothing but the truth!

Rule of Three Speech Examples

Examples of the Rule of Three can be found in some of the most famous speeches ever delivered:

- *"Veni, vidi, vici"* (I came, I saw, I conquered) – Shakespeare's Julius Caesar
- *"Friends, Romans, Countrymen. Lend me your ears"* - Shakespeare's Julius Caesar
- *"Government of the people, by the people, for the people"* - Abraham Lincoln's Gettysburg Address
- *"where the strong are just, and the weak secure and the peace preserved"* - J F Kennedy's inaugural speech
- *"There are three kinds of lies: lies, damned lies, and statistics"* – Benjamin Disraeli
- *"Our priorities are Education, Education, Education"* – Tony Blair
- *"It's been a long time coming, but tonight, because of what we did on this day, In this election, at this defining moment, change has come to America"* - Barack Obama's inaugural speech

With the example above, Obama could have simply stated:

> *"It's been a long time coming, but tonight, change is coming to America."*

They essentially say the same thing, but which has the greater impact?

The above quotation is from Obama's first election victory speech in 2008. He used the 'Rule of Three' 29 times in his 10-minute election victory speech. He used the same technique again in his 2012 election victory speech. Examples are:

"Thank you for believing all the way, through every hill, through every valley".

"You'll hear the determination in the voice ...., You'll hear the pride in the voice...................., You'll hear the deep patriotism in the voice........"

"We want our children to live in an America that isn't burdened by debt, that isn't weakened by inequality, that isn't threatened by the destructive power of a warming planet".

"We believe in a generous America, in a compassionate America, in a tolerant America".

"We have the courage to keep reaching, to keep working, to keep fighting".

Obama also used the Rule of Three in his inaugural address in January 2013. Examples are:

We, the people, still believe that.....

We, the people, still believe that......

We, the people, still believe that.....

"That is our generation's task – to make these words, these rights, these values....."

To have greater impact in presentations, it is not only what you say but how you say it.

In summary, to simplify your message, think in terms of three when drafting the content for your next presentation; identify three key messages to gain maximum impact. The Latin phrase "Omne Trium Perfectum" translates as "everything that comes in threes is perfect".

If it is good enough for the US President in his high profile speeches, then perhaps we should consider using the ‘Rule of Three’ technique in our own presentations. Using The Rule of Three is powerful!

Chapter 8
USE OF HUMOUR

Make 'em Laugh

TECHNIQUES

USE OF HUMOUR

Introduction

Your audience love to be entertained whilst getting the message from your presentation. Everyone loves to laugh, and if you can generate some laughter it helps you connect with your audience. Humour that relates to your presentation subject will enhance the content, the message and its retention. If you decide to use humour in your presentation, it is important to know how and when to use it. Only use humour when it supports your presentation rather than bringing it in randomly which could distract your audience. The humour has to be relevant to the subject. If humour does not fit comfortably into your presentation, then leave it out.

Humour, is certainly one of the characteristics of a successful presenter. That does not mean, however, that you should use humour in every presentation you give. It may not be your personal presenting style and it needs far more skill than simply just peppering your presentation with jokes.

Laughter is infectious and some presenters feel that they should tell some jokes right at the beginning to enliven their presentation. It is much more effective to tell a humourous story that introduces the subject of your presentation. Simply telling jokes which are not connected to your presentation topic can confuse your audience, especially if you are presenting on a serious subject. It will not help you give a great opening.

KEY TIP

Ensure that the humour is actually funny and helps deliver your message. If not, then leave it out.

Here are some suggestions of using humour to give greater impact to your presentations:

Personal Experiences

The best source of humour for a presentation is from your own personal experience. Try and recall an embarrassing incident that was certainly not funny at the time it happened – we all have them! Upon reflection however, you can laugh at the embarrassing incident. The best humour comes from your own personal experience. Talk about an awkward situation you experienced and the lesson learned from it. Audiences love personal stories, especially when humour is included; they help build rapport. Audiences respond to what they relate to; they can probably relate your story to their own similar experiences, so they will connect with you. Using your own experiences will provide greater impact. You can describe the incident with conviction and enthusiasm because it actually happened to you.

Some presenters use jokes they have previously heard or extract them from the internet. The danger is that audiences may have heard these jokes before and they will therefore have less impact. Furthermore, you are less likely to offend anyone if you are recalling your own personal experiences.

Is it Funny?

Before deciding to use 'humour' ask yourself honestly if you find it funny. If it does not make you laugh, then why would your audience laugh? Only consider including humour that you consider to be funny. Ensure that the humour enhances the message. Do not use humour just to be funny. We all love to laugh but it has to be in context. After telling your humorous story, pause if you get a laugh – never continue speaking over laughter. Never laugh at your own humour. If you do not hear any laughter (it happens!), do not try to explain the anecdote; just stay calm and carry on presenting. Afterwards, you can ask yourself was the lack of laughs due to your delivery, was the story out of context, or was it simply not funny?

Many presenters start by saying, *"Let me tell you an interesting story"* or in this case *"Let me tell you a funny story."* You may deem it interesting or funny, but let the audience make up their own mind.

Will the Audience get it?

Knowing your audience in advance of your presentation is very beneficial. You can tailor your presentation to meet their specific needs. This is also true when considering the use of humour. Before deciding on your humour, think about the make-up of your audience. For example, their age group, their background and how they would respond to your humour. For example, references to local schools would perhaps not be understood by people outside your area.

Beware!

You want your humour to improve your presentation, make it more enjoyable for your audience and enhance your reputation as a presenter. Ensure your humour does not have the opposite effect. Avoid offensive material at all costs. Carefully consider the use of political or religious jokes. Half of your audience may enjoy the humour but is it worth it, if you offend the other half.

When to Use Humour

Humour is best used to illustrate a point. Humour can be far more effective when demonstrating ideas than using facts and figures. Humour can be used in different ways, from funny quotes or examples, to an amusing prop, a funny picture or cartoon or an amusing anecdote. Humour helps the audience remember your point.

Enjoy it!

It is difficult to make your audience laugh if you are standing rigid and appear serious - so try and look as if you are enjoying yourself. As for all aspects of presenting, your body language plays an important part. Have fun and enjoy it.

KEY TIP

Use humour to enhance your presentation and your reputation, but never use any offensive material.

The Benefits

Some of the benefits of using humour effectively, include:

- Breaks down barriers and your audience become more receptive to your message
- Helps relax your audience and puts them at ease and in a receptive mood. If you can make them laugh they will be more engaged
- Helps to sustain your audience's attention and interest
- Can enliven a potentially dull or boring presentation say, one full of facts and figures
- Can ease tension and help when answering a difficult question
- Unites people - humour based on shared experience brings your audience together, e.g. work-place humour
- Can enhance your reputation as a presenter

If you can add humour to your presentations, you will enhance your ability to influence your audience. No one wants to sit through a boring presentation. If you can generate some laughter throughout your presentation, even when presenting a serious subject, you will hold your audience's attention and they will be more likely to stay engaged. Present your humour with confidence, enthusiasm, and happy facial expressions.

As for all presentations, rehearsal is a must; the timing and delivery of your humour are vital – Preparation, Preparation, Preparation! Your humour must be delivered spontaneously. For example, if you have to look down at your notes for the punch line, your delivery will suffer, as will the humourous impact. Your humour will fall flat.

Humour is simply another method of getting your message across, and it can help you be a better presenter. As you develop as a presenter, start to include humour in your skill set as a tool to further improve your presentations.

Chapter 9
IMPROMPTU SPEAKING

When Presenting

DEVELOPING YOUR SKILLS

IMPROMPTU SPEAKING – WHEN PRESENTING

Introduction

Impromptu speaking or, in other words, 'thinking on your feet' makes many people nervous, even fairly experienced presenters. Impromptu speaking is when you are called upon to make a speech or presentation with little or no advance warning. The scheduled speaker might be late and you are asked to step in, you could be asked to give a toast at a family or work event, or you are a member of a panel answering questions from the audience.

Here are some techniques that are widely used and can be deployed to help structure your impromptu presentation:

PEP (Position, Explain, Position)

- Position: State your position
- Explain: Your point
- Position: Restate your position

PREP (Point, Reason, Example, Point)

- *Point:* Begin by clearly outlining your point
- *Reason:* Then give your reason or reasons
- *Example:* Give examples to support and justify your point
- *Point:* Conclude by summarising your main point

Past, Present, Future

- Reflect on a past issue. For example, *"In the past the solution to the problem we face was X….*
- As of *now*, we have Y remedies to the problem….
- In *the future* we predict we will have Z solutions to the problem….

Before, the Event, the Result

- *Before* 2015 the Team Meetings were a great forum to attend
- Then in 2015 the rules were changed (*The Event*)
- The *result* was disastrous! Presentation Skills Training was introduced and we had to do impromptu speaking!

Cause, Effect, Remedy

- The *cause* of the problem we face today is X
- The *effect* of the problem is Y
- The *remedy* for the problem is Z

KEY TIP

An impromptu speech is like a mini speech so therefore should have an Opening, Body and Ending.

Issue, Pros v Cons, Conclusions

- Begin by outlining the issue

- Talk about the benefits, and then discuss the downside
- Conclude with your recommendation

Good, Bad, Indifferent

- What you believe is *good* about the subject
- What you believe is *bad*
- And *indifferent*

The 5 'W's

With this technique, you cover your subject by including the Who, What, When, Where and Why. For example, if you have been asked to talk about a club you are a member of, your structure would be:

- *Who* started it and *who* is involved now
- *What* the club goals are
- *When* it was founded
- *Where* does it take place?
- *Why* you are a member

Impromptu Speaking Delivery

Along with the above suggested techniques, here are some pointers to help your delivery:

- Speaking quickly will increase any nervous feelings you may have. Take your time. When invited to speak get up from your seat slowly.

- Stand tall. Stand on both feet about a shoulder width apart. If you can think about a clock, stand on five to one; this will help you feel more grounded and look authoritative.

- Feel and look confident. Engage your audience, smile and pause. Resist the urge to slump your shoulders, put your hands in your pockets, sway or look away from your audience. Speak and behave in a confident manner.

- Take your time to begin. Before you speak, engage with your audience by looking around the room and making eye contact with them. Smile whilst doing this.

- Use the power of the pause and never be afraid of the silence. Remember time appears slower to you than your audience. Pauses are welcomed by audiences. They will think you are gathering your thoughts or allowing them time to reflect on your previous point.

- Paraphrase or restate the subject or question. This gives you some thinking time and ensures that you will answer the correct question.

- Use your notes (if you had time to make some) as an aid-memoire. Do not try to remember everything. If you forget, you will become more nervous. Instead, talk through the points you noted as a mini speech.

- Select one key message and focus on that. As you speak, you may think of other ideas. If this happens, just go with the flow and see what comes out.

- Be brief. As you did not have any time to prepare, your audience will not be expecting you to say too much. Audiences are more likely to listen if you avoid rambling.

- Imagine that your impromptu speaking is a one to one conversation with a friend. This will help you to relax.

- Personalise your speech. Use examples from your own experience so it is much easier to speak because the event actually happened to you. Using personal stories engages your audience and gives you credibility.

- Ask the audience if they have any questions or comments. This will give you time to gather your thoughts.

- To close, summarise your points briefly and if possible, make your final remark the key message – finish on a high.

Remember the following when you are engaged in impromptu speaking:

Structure

Try to structure your impromptu session with an Opening, a Body and an Ending (OBE). Choose a maximum of three key points to present so that the audience will retain your message. Use the time you have between being asked to speak and actually standing up to deliver to plan your talk, even if the time is limited.

Language

Use words that your audience will understand, do not speak over their heads. You are not there to show your command of the English language; you are there to get your message across to your audience. Be careful of using jargon – will your audience understand it?

Vocal Variety

Use your voice to engage your audience, speaking softly or loudly, and with expression (Refer to the Vocal Variety chapter).

Body Language

Use gestures to enhance and reinforce what you are saying (Refer to the Body Language chapter).

Practice

The ability to quickly think on your feet and speak is an asset and will help develop confidence in your presentation skills. To develop the skill, start to practice by speaking for two minutes on a chosen subject. Start with easy subjects, ones you are familiar with and then move on to more challenging topics.

> *"It usually takes more than three weeks to prepare a good impromptu speech."*

Mark Twain

Chapter 10

IMPROMPTU SPEAKING

How To Be More Effective At Meetings

DEVELOPING YOUR SKILLS

IMPROMPTU SPEAKING – HOW TO BE MORE EFFECTIVE AT MEETINGS

Introduction

We are often put on the spot. Whether it is during a team meeting, presenting the annual budget or business plan, if your boss suddenly asks for your view or, when you have to handle questions after a presentation. The ability to articulate your thoughts in these situations is a skill. When you achieve this skill, it injects immediate confidence in what you are saying. You become more credible, the foundation of leadership.

Here are 6 tips to help you 'think on your feet' at meetings:

Number 1: Actively Listen

Listening is critical to thinking on your feet. You need to listen actively in order to fully understand the question or request before you reply. If you respond too quickly, you risk giving an unnecessary or even an inappropriate response. To help you with your listening, remember to:

- Look directly at the questioner
- Observe the body language as well as the words

Number 2: Have the Question Repeated

You can ask for the question to be repeated. This provides you with additional time to consider how you wish to reply. People sometimes think that this makes them appear hesitant. On the contrary, it shows you are keen to provide an appropriate response. It also gives the questioner an opportunity to rephrase the question. The questioner may only have just thought about the question, so when you ask them to repeat it, it gives them a second opportunity to clarify their own thoughts and express their request more effectively.

Number 3: Plan Your Answers

It is often possible to predict the types of questions that may come up, therefore you can prepare and rehearse your answers. For example, when you are presenting the business update, the sales figures, or the sales pipeline at the Sales Review meeting. Your update will probably trigger most of the obvious questions you would expect to be asked, but what other questions might be raised? Is there anything exceptional about this month's update? What new questions might be asked as a result? What response would you give? What additional data would you need to bring to the update meeting, to support any more detailed questions?

Spend some preparation time considering the most challenging questions that participants might ask, then prepare and rehearse good answers to them. Preparation, preparation, preparation!

KEY TIP

Try and anticipate the questions that may be posed. Then prepare and practice your answers.

Number 4: Practice Your Delivery

How you say something is almost as important as what you say. If you appear unsure, mumble or frequently use 'Um' or 'Ah', the participants will lose confidence in you and question your credibility. To overcome this, try using the following techniques:

- Speak in a strong and assertive voice
- Use vocal variety. Vary your pitch and pace and consider how your message will be received. Use a lower pitch when making an important point
- Use pauses to emphasise a point or to ensure the participants get your point

- Remember to use appropriate body language
- Be aware of any jargon or technical terms. Will your audience understand what you are saying? One way of measuring your success is how much your audience understand
- When preparing and practising your responses, modify your words until they flow smoothly and easily

Number 5: Stay Calm

It is important to remain calm at all times when being queried or challenged at meetings. Always respond in a polite, positive and professional manner. Refer back to the facts that you have used in your update to support your position. Do not assume that the questioner heard these or realised their significance. The questioner may have misunderstood, been distracted or left the meeting at that point.

Number 6: Summarise

Conclude your update or response with a quick summation and then resist adding any further information. Silence may follow, but never be afraid of the silence. Do not make the common mistake of filling the silence with more information! The participants are assimilating your update. If you add more details, you may confuse them, say something unintended or start further unnecessary discussion and diminish your great update delivery.

Use transitions (outlined in the Structure chapter) to indicate that you are summarising e.g. 'in conclusion', 'finally' or you can briefly restate the question and your answer – *"what did I do to analyse the sales pipeline? I reviewed the top ten customers and prepared a thorough sales forecast."*

Chapter 11

LISTENING SKILLS

Listen Look And Learn

COMMUNICATION

LISTENING SKILLS

Introduction

Listening is the ability to accurately receive and interpret messages and is vital for effective communication including presentations and meetings. Hearing is one of our five senses. Listening is a skill that requires focus, patience and practice.

In order to understand the message we must listen effectively. Listening means concentrating not only on the message, but how it is expressed in terms of the language used, the vocal variety and the body language.

In oral communication, listening plays an important role. Listening is paying attention and responding accordingly. A good listener is proactive rather than passive; they ask questions and validate the facts.

Active Listening

Listening can be difficult at times, which is why effective listening is often termed active listening. Active listening has a number of benefits:

- You receive the message the speaker intended
- Creates a better understanding and rapport between the speaker and listener
- You learn more
- Leads to better decisions
- Avoids misunderstanding, as people confirm that they do understand what has been communicated
- Provides the best feed back to the speaker

KEY TIP

Listening requires focus and attention. Listening means concentrating not only on the words, but how they are spoken, the use of language and body language. Be aware of both the verbal and non-verbal messages.

Key Elements

Here are some tips to improve active listening which will help to ensure that you really hear the other person's message, and that the other person knows you are receiving precisely what they say:

Focus and Really Listen

To actively listen, give your undivided attention to the presenter:

- Look at the presenter directly and give them your full attention
- Avoid distractions – this means the environment and your thoughts
- Avoid being distracted by conversations on the side with colleagues, when listening in a group
- Allow the person to speak, without mentally preparing a rebuttal
- Show empathy by being open to the speaker's ideas and sensitive to their values and feelings - see things from the speaker's perspective
- Keep an open mind to what is being said. Wait until the speaker is finished before deciding that you disagree
- If the speaker hesitates, encourage them to conclude rather than start your reply
- Do not interrupt – let the speaker finish

- Pause to reflect on what has been said and then formulate your response
- Pay attention to the presenter's body language

Demonstrate That You Are Listening

Use your body language and gestures to show that you are actively listening:

- Nod to acknowledge what is being said
- Smile and use other facial expressions
- Use eye contact to show you are interested in what is being said and that you have connected with the presenter
- Encourage the presenter with small verbal comments such as 'yes'
- Have an open, inviting and interested posture

If you demonstrate that you value what the speaker has to say they, in turn, are more likely to listen to you.

Paraphrase and Question

As the listener, your job is to understand what is being said. It is therefore useful to occasionally paraphrase what the speaker has said. Paraphrasing helps you to clarify what the other person said and allows the speaker to resolve any misunderstandings, e.g. "*What I'm hearing is.....*", "*It sounds like what you are saying is........*"

Another technique is to ask questions in order to clarify points. Open ended questions that are short, objective, direct and do not include an answer within the question are best. For example, instead of saying *"Don't you think we should go ahead and have presentation skills training?"* you could reframe it and ask *"What do you think we should do about presentation skills training?"* Asking questions shows the speaker that you are interested in what s/he has to say, as well as perhaps obtaining additional information before you reply.

If you are communicating something really important, it can be useful to ask questions of the person you are communicating with, to ensure that they fully understand.

Paraphrasing and questioning ensures the intended communication is received and understood.

Feedback through Body Language

You need feedback, otherwise you cannot be certain that your listeners have understood your message. Sometimes feedback can be verbal, or it can be through body language. The previous paragraph discussed the importance of asking questions and listening carefully. However, feedback through body language is perhaps even more revealing when measuring the effectiveness of your communication. By watching the facial expressions, gestures and posture of your listeners, you will learn their:

- Confidence levels
- Understanding (or the lack of it)
- Agreement with what you are saying
- Defensiveness
- Level of engagement with your subject
- Level of interest
- Honesty (or the lack of it!)

When you are presenting, if you understand your audiences' body language, you can adapt your presentation to make it clearer, more engaging and relevant.

As a listener, body language can tell you more about what the speaker is saying. As previously advised, you can then ask questions to ensure that you have understood each other and thus avoid any misunderstanding.

Suspend Judgement

Interrupting wastes everyone's time. It can also frustrate the presenter and adversely impact the understanding of the message.

To avoid the above:

- Allow the speaker to finish each point before asking questions
- Do not interrupt with counter arguments

Respond with Respect

By actively listening you are getting information and insight. You achieve nothing by attacking the speaker or being derogatory. You should:

- Be open and honest in your response
- State your opinions respectfully
- Treat the other person as he or she would want to be treated and how you would expect to be treated yourself

KEY TIP

People want to feel valued, appreciated and respected; they want to feel understood. If you respect them they will reciprocate and respect you.

Never be Afraid of the Silence

As for our formal presentations, we often do not enjoy silence in conversations. So we find ways to fill the gaps. Using silence, however, encourages the speaker to continue talking, to expand on the points, or to be more revealing than they perhaps meant to be. When you use silence effectively you will hear and learn more.

Summary

Listening is a skill. You must concentrate to be an active listener. Your goal is to truly hear what the other person is saying. It is not about hearing what you want to hear. Avoid all distractions and focus on the message. Ask questions and paraphrase to ensure you understand the message. Remember that the key to achieving results is not merely to talk, but to listen, and actively listen. So challenge yourself to become an active listener!

Chapter 12

HOW TO HANDLE A Q&A SESSION

Reinforce Your Message, Not Undermine It

COMMUNICATION

HOW TO HANDLE A Q&A SESSION

Introduction

A great Question and Answer (Q&A) session is one that adds value to your presentation. It requires careful planning and thoughtful contributions from both the audience and the presenter. However, too many presentations fall flat when it comes to the Q&A and the audience leave with unanswered questions.

The skills outlined in the Impromptu Speaking chapters, will prove invaluable in handling your Q&As professionally.

Answering questions from your audience can help you be more effective as a presenter. The Q&A session can depict you as confident, professional and in control. The session can reinforce your depth of subject knowledge and improve the engagement between you and your audience - but only if you can handle it successfully. How you conduct the Q&A session will influence your audience's overall judgement of you, your credibility and your presentation. An effective Q&A session should only add value to your presentation and to you as a presenter.

It is often argued that presenters should never say *"that's a good question"* when a question is posed by a member of the audience. I believe it is a good technique to use, albeit sparingly, as it signals to your audience that you genuinely welcome questions. It also compliments the questioner and makes them feel good. Furthermore, it gives you time to think of your response.

The Q&A session can be seen as an impromptu session with a number of 'think on your feet' topics. This potentially, makes it more challenging than your actual presentation, which you have been able to thoroughly prepare for. Outlined below are some techniques on how to successfully handle Q&A sessions. Please note that these guidelines are applicable at formal presentations and also at any meetings you chair or attend as a participant.

1. Preparation Preparation Preparation!

You have thoroughly prepared for your presentation and really know your content. Now try and predict what questions your audience could possibly ask, where might they want more detail and prepare and practice your answers prior to your presentation. Furthermore, consider how you will refer back to your presentation as you answer the question. This reinforces the message of your presentation and helps maintain the focus of the Q&A session.

As part of your preparation, be sure to include time for the Q&A session.

KEY TIP

Be aware that many speaking situations can involve two presentations: the formal presentation followed by the Q&A session. Ensure success with both presentations by thorough preparation.

2. Establish the Rules

Let your audience know at the beginning of your presentation when you will be taking questions. By informing your audience of the format, you establish a level of authority and retain control of the situation.

Some presenters welcome questions throughout a presentation. Most, however, prefer to handle questions near the end. If you take questions near the end, be sure to inform your audience that there will be a Q&A. If you inform them at the beginning that they will have a chance to ask questions, they can begin to think of relevant questions during your talk. Taking questions at the end, helps avoid the audience interruptions that sometimes make a presentation difficult to follow or causes it to run over time. It also helps the presenter to concentrate on their delivery, free of interruption, which can be helpful especially for inexperienced presenters.

Make sure you set aside time for the Q&A session if you have informed your audience that there will be one.

3. Listen and Be Attentive

When you begin your Q&As be inviting and encouraging as many members of your audience will have questions but may be afraid to stand up in public and ask them. While listening to the question look at the questioner and smile. Engage with them. You might nod to show that you are listening. Nodding does not mean that you agree with their opinion. It simply shows that you are listening and you understand.

Listen to the complete question before you begin your answer. Too often, people start answering before the whole question is even asked. This can result in giving a response which had nothing to do with the question. Ensure you listen to the complete question to fully understand it in order to be able to answer it.

If the person seems to be rambling or asks a lengthy question, you can politely interrupt with *"And your question is?"* Be sure to smile when you say this, otherwise it may be perceived as discourteous.

When asked an irrelevant question, be polite and acknowledge the interest of the question. Then advise that as it is not strictly relevant to the main subject, you would be happy to meet the questioner after the session, to discuss his/her question on a one-to-one basis.

4. Restate or Reframe

Engage with the person asking the question and smile and invite them to stand up to ask their question. After the question has been asked, pause for a few seconds then restate the question while looking at the entire audience. This is done to:

- Ensure the entire audience has heard and understood the question and therefore will understand your response. It is frustrating for an audience member to hear the answer but not the question

- Demonstrate to the questioner that you heard the question

- Provide you with some time to consider your response should you need it. It may be only a few seconds but that can be sufficient to prepare a good response

Having said the above, there are occasions when you may not want to repeat the question. Instead you reframe it. This is done because:

- The question was long and rambling
- The question, or the words used, were offensive
- You do not want to answer the question the way it was worded

5. Pause

After you have repeated or reframed the question, pause for a few seconds. This allows the audience to think about the question and therefore the value of your answer. In addition, the audience will be ready to digest your answer after they have had a few seconds to process the question.

Unless it is an easy question with a simple factual answer, the presenter can pause and consider possible answers. Audiences are not expecting immediate answers to difficult questions. After a pause, your answer should be more coherent.

6. Answer and Involve

It is important to remember that although you are answering a question from one member of the audience, you are still responsible for the interest and engagement of all. Begin answering by engaging with the questioner by making eye contact and then extend eye contact to the rest of your audience. It is the entire audience who should hear your answer and not just the person who asked the question. If you are close to the person when they started their question, move away from them in order to take in as many of the audience as possible. You want to include the whole audience in the discussion, otherwise they will switch off.

As you conclude your answer, look back at the questioner; their body language, in particular their facial expression, indicates whether you have answered their question satisfactorily.

If you felt that you answered the question well you can ask the questioner, "*Does that answer your question?*" You usually get a positive response.

On the other hand, if you felt that you answered the question poorly, do not make eye contact with the questioner. This may encourage them to ask a follow-up question or challenge your poor answer. Instead, look to another part of the room and invite the next question.

7. Be Brief

Answer questions in a thorough yet short, concise and simple manner, when possible. Do not take too long and risk boring your audience. Be succinct in your answers. It may be that the only person really interested in the answer, is the one who asked the question! However, resist answering with a terse response as this may come across as discourteous. If it is a complex question, answer as concisely as possible and then offer to discuss in more detail after the session, if they are interested.

8. The Domineering Questioner

Do not let your Q&A session be dominated by a few audience members. If you observe this happening, you could say "*We've heard from this side of the room*" and move to the other side of the room and say "*Let's hear from this side of the room*". Alternatively, you could ask if anyone has a different viewpoint to contribute. Be warned – the domineering questioner usually turns up!

9. Be Fair

Give everyone a chance to ask a question irrespective of where they are seated and do not just invite those with a friendly face. An audience member who has not asked a question so far, should have preference over one who already has.

10. Honesty is the best Policy!

People are frustrated hearing, for example football managers, players or politicians being interviewed and evading the questions. If you do not know the answer to a question, be honest and say so, but offer to get back to the questioner with an answer later on. Your audience will appreciate your honesty and respect you for it. Alternatively, if you do not know the answer, you could ask if anyone in the audience knows. Never stumble your way through an answer; if it proves to be wrong, it can dent your credibility.

KEY TIP

If you have been asked a question take responsibility to deal with it; your goal is to leave no question unanswered.

11. Self Control

It is important to always be polite to your audience and always stay calm, no matter how challenging you are finding the Q&A session. If you lose your composure there is a risk that you may say something that you will regret. The difficulty may be as a result of the questions or the questioners. Show courtesy by listening intently and treating every question with the respect it deserves. When in doubt about the intentions of the questioner, always remain positive - your audience will appreciate this. Do not argue or become defensive when answering questions. You can sometimes encounter a member of the audience who strongly disagrees with you. This is not the time to get into a debate. Politely say, "*I appreciate your point of view, thank you*" and then invite the next question. A questioner may get away with insulting you, but you will not get away with insulting a questioner.

KEY TIP

Stay calm and in control no matter what the motive of the questioner appears to be. Never be rude to any member of your audience.

12. Opening and Closing the Session

Sometimes no one in the audience wants to be the first person to ask a question. To overcome this, ask the first question yourself. For example you could say, *"One of the questions I'm often asked is "......"*.

When starting your Q&A session, do not say, *"Do you have any questions?"* Some may interpret that statement to mean they were not listening or did not understand your message. It is far more effective to ask, *"What questions do you now have?"* or *"Who has the first question?"* People are encouraged by this subtle change and become more willing to ask questions, as they feel that you are expecting them.

Close the Q&A session after you have answered a number of questions or as you approach the agreed time limit. Ideally, wait until you give an excellent answer to a question, and then inform your audience that, regretfully, you have run out of time. If no questions bring excellent answers, end by saying, "*We're just about out of time for questions, but many of you are probably still wondering........*" and then insert a question of your own that you can follow up with a strong answer. Finish on a high!

KEY TIP

Start your Q&A session by asking *"What questions do you have?"* or *"Who has the first question?"*

13. When to Have the Q&As

It is very common for presenters to finish their presentation with a Q&A session. However, the final moments of your presentation are too important to be potentially ruined by the Q&A, as you sometimes have limited control over the Q&A session. By leaving your Q&A until the end, your credibility and the 'lasting impression' we all strive for can be adversely affected by the final question. Invariably, the last question is the one you had hoped would not be asked! People remember longest the last thing they hear.

You have thoroughly prepared your presentation's conclusion and therefore, it is likely, to be more effective if you hold your Q&A session before your conclusion. This way, you ensure that you finish your presentation on your own terms – you can finish on a high! You could say the following:

"We now have 10 minutes for questions and then I'll conclude the session."

Your audience will then know that the Q&A is not the end of your session, so will not start to pack up and disturb proceedings. Your audience's expectations are clearly set up and you will finish with greater impact.

KEY TIP

Have your Q&A session before the ending of your presentation. Handle the questions and then conclude your presentation. Finish on a high!

Conclusion

Be aware that many speaking occasions can involve two presentations: the formal presentation followed by the Q&A session (thinking on your feet). Ensure success with both presentations by using the techniques described above for the question and answer session. Please also refer to the chapters '***Impromptu Speaking – Presenting***' and '***Impromptu Speaking – How to be More Effective at Meetings***'.

Handling questions from your audience is an integral part of your presentation and can determine the success (or failure) of your overall performance. It shows that you are knowledgeable and not 'just' a presenter. Preparation is key, so be prepared! Preparation, Preparation, Preparation!

Chapter 13

EVALUATE TO MOTIVATE

Benefiting Both The Speaker And Evaluator

USEFUL TOOLS & RESOURCES

EVALUATE TO MOTIVATE

Introduction

There are times when we are asked by friends or colleagues to give feedback on their presentations. This can be as part of their preparation, or after they have given a formal presentation. There are a number of evaluation techniques available which can provide the speaker with useful information and insight. The feedback will also encourage them to carry on performing presentations. The more effective we are at evaluating each other, the more each one of us will gain from the experience.

As the evaluator, you learn to improve your listening and impromptu speaking skills. Furthermore, when you learn to evaluate others, you can apply the same objective evaluation skills to your own presentations.

As the presenter, the benefits of effective evaluations include:

- **Immediate Feedback** - Receiving constructive feedback and helpful advice soon after your presentation, helps to reinforce your positive skills and provides guidance on areas that need further improvement.

- **Improvement Suggestions** – Sometimes, when assessing your own performance, you miss some of the concerns, or choose to ignore them. An evaluator however can offer a new and independent viewpoint and will commend your strong points and suggest recommendations in those areas that require improvement.

- **Confidence** - As you work on the feedback and improve as a presenter, you grow in confidence. This growth in confidence also benefits you in your professional and personal relationships.

You should see the evaluator as a catalyst for change. As an evaluator, your role is to provide the presenter with feedback that can be used to improve and fine tune their performance. Whether or not the presenter acts on your feedback is up to them.

How to Evaluate Effectively

There are 6 principal points to consider when offering your evaluation:

Number 1: Here to Help

As an evaluator your main purpose is to help and encourage the presenter. You therefore need to clearly demonstrate that you are interested in both the presentation as well as the presenter's ability to learn, grow and develop. Your efforts are focused on helping the presenter. Keep an open mind and actively listen and observe.

Your challenge is to highlight both the strengths and areas for improvement in the presentation you have just observed. You should do this in a helpful, encouraging and sincere manner that will motivate the presenter to present again. Do not end their presenting career before it even takes off!

Number 2: Presenter's Objectives

The ability to evaluate a presentation that you have just observed is challenging and requires organisation and preparation. If feasible, contact the presenter in advance to:

- Review, discuss and clarify the presentation objectives
- Establish any concerns regarding the presentation or the presenter's speaking abilities

You need to consider the presenter's individual needs, goals and their level of experience when preparing to evaluate. For example, is this their first presentation or are they fairly experienced?

You may not have time to cover all the points identified in your evaluation. If time is limited, you should select two or three points which you feel are most important in terms of improving the presentation and expand on them.

Number 3: Personalise your Language

Carefully consider how you will present your feedback. The presenter has probably put a lot of time and effort into preparing and practising their presentation and now anxiously waits for your feedback. You must, therefore, carefully consider your language. For example, instead of using phrases such as:

"*You didn't.........*"

"*You should have.........*"

"*It's disappointing that you.........*"

"*You failed to.........*"

Think about your role and purpose as an evaluator which is to encourage and suggest improvement. Instead of the above, consider saying the following:

"*I believe.........*"

"*My reaction was.........*"

"*I feel that..........*"

"*I suggest that..........*"

Always use positive language even when offering recommendations for improvement. As an evaluator, consider the following when structuring your evaluation:

What I saw

What I heard

What I felt

Remember that you are expressing your own opinion and not the audience's (if there is one). You can only accurately share your observations, thoughts and feelings. You should therefore start with 'I' and not 'we' as if speaking on behalf of the audience.

Number 4: Evaluate the Presentation - Not the Presenter

Be aware that your feedback can upset or cause emotional responses from the person you are evaluating.

As an evaluator, always be mindful of your main purpose which is to support, help and encourage the presenter. Do not try to impose your views on the presenter. Instead of evaluating the presenter's ideas for their quality, your aim is to help the presenter communicate their thoughts more effectively, whether you agree with them or not.

Furthermore, your feedback should be about the presenter's delivery not about the presenter as a person. This enables a positive exchange that helps the presenter to grow and develop without being judged on a personal level. Keep your feedback focused on the presentation.

KEY TIP

Evaluate what the speaker does – not what the speaker is.

Number 5: Promote Self Confidence

As an evaluator, you must seek to encourage and inspire the presenter to perform again. Give honest and sincere commendations, positive reinforcement when improvements are observed and helpful recommendations. Always end your evaluation on a positive note in order to help build self-esteem and self-confidence. Finally, you could sign off by saying *"and I very much look forward to your next presentation."*

After your evaluation, the presenter should feel positive and motivated to continue to perform more presentations.

Number 6: Be Truthful

Evaluators can sometimes only commend and offer no recommendations. This is easy for them but not very helpful to the presenter. This type of feedback does not provide the presenter with any suggested improvements, thereby limiting their ability to grow. Honest evaluations can, and must, be positive and encouraging but must include suggested improvements. Be honest in your evaluation, anything less will be valueless and can damage your credibility and reputation.

Even when you are not asked to be an evaluator, you should still give feedback. The more feedback a presenter receives, the more they benefit. Presenters welcome feedback, it helps us improve. Your feedback does not need to be as detailed as that of the assigned evaluator, but it should include something the presenter did well, areas that could be improved and a specific recommendation for improvement.

Listen and Learn

When you are the presenter receiving an evaluation, carefully consider each comment and suggestion for improvement. Do not immediately dismiss the feedback by thinking, *"This evaluator does not know what s/he is talking about,"* or *"They have missed the point completely"* - you may be dismissing some valuable feedback and opportunity to improve.

Remember, the evaluator is simply offering their opinion of what they saw, heard and felt – perception is reality! Some of their opinions and observations may be justified and it will make you a better presenter if you incorporate them into your next presentation.

KEY TIP

Listen carefully to the feedback, digest it and then decide if you wish to use it.

Summary

Evaluating is an important learning tool and skill to develop. When you evaluate you are improving your own skills as a presenter and, also helping the presenter achieve their own development goals. The skills you learn and develop can be applied in all aspects of your life; you can become a better listener and a more critical thinker.

Aim to provide a positive, constructive, insightful and encouraging evaluation which you and the presenter will benefit from.

See the Preparation Checklist/Evaluation Guide on the next page to help you cover the key points when structuring your evaluation. The guide can also be used as a checklist when preparing a presentation to ensure that you have covered the key points for a successful performance.

PREPARATION CHECKLIST/ EVALUATION GUIDE

Presenter ______________________ Presentation Title ______________________

Objectives ______________________

Date of Presentation ______________________

Area	Key Pointers	Presenter's Comment/ Evaluator Feedback
Organisation		
Preparation	Evidence of preparation, research.	
Purpose	Clear. To Inform, Persuade, Inspire or Entertain. Were presentation objectives met?	
Use of notes (if any)	Notes not intrusive. Notes effectively managed. Hindered delivery.	
Structure	Structured outline used. Logical flow, Opening leading to Body leading to Ending.	
Opening	Grabbed the audience attention and engaged them.	
Body	Sustained interest. Easy to follow – good sign posting.	
Ending	Made an impact. Memorable. Good summary. Call to action.	
Vocal Variety	Pitch, Pace, Pause, Projection, Passion, Posture & Practice.	
Pitch	Varied – not monotonous.	
Pace	Well paced and varied throughout. Not rushed.	
Pause	Used effectively to get message across. Used at appropriate points.	

Area	Key Pointers	Presenter's Comment/ Evaluator Feedback
Projection	Clear, audible and good articulation.	
Passion	Appeared passionate. Showed genuine interest in message.	
Posture	Appeared confident. No slouched or slumped shoulders.	
Practice	Evidence of preparation through good delivery.	
Body Language	Relaxed, controlled, confident, appropriate movements and gestures. Enhanced the presentation. No slouching or swaying.	
Stance	Upper body movement. Whole body movement.	
Hand Gestures	Gestures support/enhance the spoken word. Not a distraction.	
Facial Expression	Serious, pleasant, friendly, nervous, engaging, rapport. Smile. Expression supported message.	
Eye Contact	Sustained, continuous, engaging. Not just fleeting glances.	
Delivery	Impact on audience. Authority. Credible. Engaging. Displayed confidence. No Ums and Ahs. Language appropriate for audience. No jargon used. Humour used effectively.	
Q&A Session	Handled effectively.	
Timing	Within time allocation. Exceeded time. Too short.	

Area	Key Pointers	Presenter's Comment/ Evaluator Feedback
Appearance	Dressed and groomed appropriately. Met audience's expectations.	
Commendation	What was done particularly well?	
Recommendation	Top three recommendations	
Overall Impression		

Chapter 14

DOs AND DON'Ts

USEFUL TOOLS & RESOURCES

DOs

Do undertake plenty of Preparation, Preparation, Preparation!

DO consider your audience – what's in it for them?

DO have a proper structure with an OBE, your opening, body and ending.

DO engage with your audience, by maintaining good, evenly distributed eye contact with them.

DO be enthusiastic showing lots of confidence and energy.

DO speak clearly and loudly enough so that everyone can comfortably hear you.

DO use vocal variety to add interest and sustain your audience's interest.

DO use transitions to enable your presentation to be delivered in a logical sequence making it easy to follow.

DO remember that it is not only what you say, but how you say it.

DO prepare for questions. Try to anticipate the types of questions that may be asked and prepare your answers.

DO finish on time – or early but never go over time.

DO seek feedback – it's the way we learn and improve.

DON'Ts

DON'T prepare too much material. Focus on three points maximum.

DON'T start with an apology.

DON'T rock, sway or use repetitive gestures.

DON'T use complex words or jargon.

DON'T read your script – a read speech is a dead speech!

DON'T use your hands to fidget with a pen or pointer.

DON'T speak in a monotonous voice.

DON'T speak too quickly – this can happen when you are feeling nervous, but it makes it difficult for your audience to understand you and highlights your nervousness.

DON'T be afraid of the silence – use pauses.

DON'T use filler words – use pauses.

DON'T forget to be verbal, visual and vocal.

DON'T be afraid to experiment.

DON'T forget to practise – Preparation, Preparation, Preparation!

Chapter 15

THE NEXT STEP

I Can And I Will

THE NEXT STEP

Thank you for reading this book. This is the end.........or the beginning.

What are you going to do next?

How do you plan to challenge yourself with your newly acquired skills?

What will you do differently?

When will you next speak or present?

Remember, it is not only what you say, but how you say it. Inexperienced presenters are inclined to concentrate on their content (what they say) without much focus on their delivery (the way they say it). Commit as much effort in preparing your delivery as your content in order to become a great presenter. Work on both your structure and delivery.

Seek opportunities to present in front of others. Try and put yourself in situations that require public speaking. Volunteer as much as you can by, for instance, presenting at team meetings or clubs you are associated with.

The best way of developing into a 'good' and then a 'great' presenter, is to practise and always seek feedback on your performance. Use the Preparation Checklist/Evaluation Guide to help you improve.

Success is rarely instant; most successful presenters have invested a lot of time and effort working towards and achieving their goals. Look, listen and learn from other presenters (TED talks are a good resource). Study their strengths and weaknesses and incorporate their effective techniques into your own speaking skills.

When you present, expect that you will feel nervous or anxious. This is part of your preparation, so do not try to eliminate your nerves totally, but aim to manage them. The best in any field are nervous, but they control their nerves and use them to their advantage. So expect those butterflies in your stomach, but get them flying in formation to provide the adrenaline to deliver a great performance. Banish all negative thoughts and replace them with positive thoughts. Visualise yourself performing your best presentation and then go out and deliver it.

Being able to deliver effective presentations is a life skill which enhances your reputation and gives you greater confidence and self-belief. The more you do it, the easier it becomes – you may even start to enjoy the experience!

KEY TIP

The only way to do it is to do it. So when do you plan to do your next presentation?

Should you require any further assistance, wish to arrange workshops for your teams or to have one-to-one coaching, please contact Patrick at Patrick.ebbs@changenable.com

For general enquiries please contact Ican@changenable.com

www.changenable.com

19920081R00059

Printed in Great Britain
by Amazon